To Al
With all
and everything a
girl you.
Love, Mom
7/17/98

If I could, I would give you...

Ellen Reilly McCormick
ILLUSTRATIONS BY WILBUR BULLOCK

CONTEMPORARY BOOKS
A TRIBUNE COMPANY

Library of Congress Cataloging-in-Publication Data

McCormick, Ellen Reilly.
    If I could, I would give you— / Ellen Reilly McCormick ;
illustrations by Wilbur Bullock.
       p.   cm.
    ISBN 0-8092-3218-9
    1. Love poetry, American.   I. Bullock, Wilbur.   II. Title.
PS3563.C344543I3   1996
811'.54—dc20   95-50473
                                                                                  CIP

Text copyright © 1996 by Ellen Reilly McCormick
Illustrations copyright © 1996 by Wilbur Bullock
All rights reserved
Published by Contemporary Books, Inc.
Two Prudential Plaza, Chicago, Illinois 60601-6790
Manufactured in the United States of America
International Standard Book Number: 0-8092-3218-9
10   9   8   7   6   5   4   3   2   1

If I could, I would give you...

Catered brunch, your place, for eight
Roses rambling on the gate
Tarot cards (predict your fate)
One perfect pearl upon your plate

Unlimited fonts and a laser printer
    Unlimited Aspen runs next winter
    The unabridged works of Harold Pinter
    The stamina of a world-class sprinter

A partner for each lonely sock
    Badminton net and shuttlecock
    Fugues, courtesy of J. S. Bach
    New pickles from a
        stoneware crock

A private audience with the Pope
    An avant garde kaleidoscope
    A printout of your horoscope
    Forget the plans—let's just elope

Acres of farmland and a plow
   Llamas, chickens, and a cow
   Apples heavy on the bough
   White lilies when we've had a row

Crampons, spikes,
   pitons, and rope
Skis and poles and
   boots and slope
Bucket, sponges, brushes, soap
A moon map and a telescope

Hand-knit warmth of glove or mitten
   Two easy chairs for friends to sit in
   A snuggly robe for two to fit in
   Fake nails (for the ones you've bitten)

Apple trees for your backyard
A book of jokes (you're such a card)
Tutu, slippers, leotard
And I will be your bodyguard

A shopping spree from hat to shoes
A Newport fest all jazz and blues
An earful of the latest news
A stack of stick-'em-on tattoos

A necklace carved from ebony
Steaming pots of oolong tea
Six hours' worth of carpentry
My vote, if you're the nominee

Your garden rototilled and seeded
　　Watered, pruned, raked, hoed, and weeded
　　A denim jacket fringed and beaded
　　A pair of hands when they are needed

Rendering of the family crest
　　Placards for your next protest
　　Virgin olive oil, cold-pressed
　　Quilted ruby velvet vest

A broker who won't churn your stocks
　　Tennis, running, hiking socks
　　A set of antique stoneware crocks
　　When you regress—alphabet blocks

Plumbing before you need it most
    A round-trip ticket to the coast
    The yard fenced in, picket or post
    Scalloped potatoes and pot roast

Thistle seed and a bird feeder
    Gloves, a trowel, a hoe, a weeder
    Two-hour lunch with your town leader
    A pedigreed kitten from a breeder

Your choice of charitable donation
    A trained-to-sit-and-stay dalmatian
    Stars and stripes to hail our nation
    A send-the-kids-to-camp vacation

Rod and reel and real live bait
   Antique lead-crystal paperweight
   A money loan, long-term, low-rate
   A CB to communicate

Snorkel, beach ball,
   inner tube
Jigsaw puzzles, Rubik's Cube
Ringside circus seats (hey, Rube!)
Car care: oil change and lube

Erasers, pencils, legal pads
   One each of the latest fads
   Two hours dusting your doodads
   Spring bulb planting: fifty glads

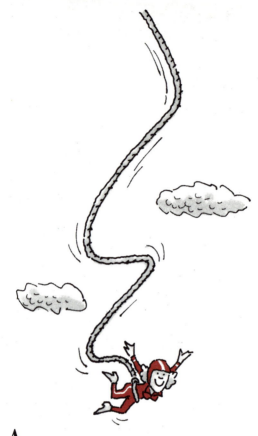

A jouncy, bouncy, bungee jump
Recycling bins instead of dump
Thighs lipo'd free of lump and bump
Next bridge hand, I won't overtrump

Willow basket filled with fruits
   Pennywhistles to toot-toots
   Double-breasted, pinstriped suits
   I'll break in your new hiking boots

Fireplace hearth, tongs, brush, and poker
   Eighteen-carat spun-gold choker
   The number of my discount broker
   Abolishment of the mediocre

A château leased. Next fall, Bordeaux?
   Wild flower seeds to reap and sow
   Tin soldiers marching row on row
   A pewter pot of hot cocoa

Carriage ride in Central Park
   Tiny dog: no bite, no bark
   Board and darts to hit the mark
   Night-light to dispel the dark

Courage when your feet hit clay
   Hair transplant (toss that toupee!)
   Breakfast on a silver tray
   I'll run the errands Saturday

A thoroughbred, white blaze and socks
Ferragamos, Birkenstocks
Shaggy dogs, puns, and knock-knocks
Seafood dinner at the docks

Bathing cap, nose plugs, lap pool
A beagle pup that doesn't drool
A framed and matted Golden Rule
I'll drive your after-school carpool

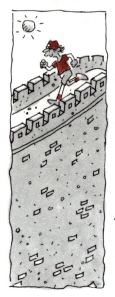

New England in the spring and fall
    A jog on China's long, long wall
    Tickets to a charity ball
    Two morns without a wake-up call

A tree, in memory of kin
    The glowing light from lanterns tin
    To dress and pose: a mannequin
    A juicy bunch of grapes, no skin

A Japanese garden, stoned and mossed
A compass so you don't get lost
A Caesar salad, dressed and tossed
Your teeth, permanently flossed

S

ervice for twelve from Royal Doulton
A long good night from John Boy Walton
A ride down roads that sped Kuralt on
Codfish dried, with half the salt on

The world's great books to read and ponder
  Skydive with a California condor
  Australia's outback you could wander
  Or rope a cow a way out yonder

Visit from Santa Claus in June
A day guarding the common loon
A teen who never answers, "Soon"
Another sweet James Taylor tune

Your family tree from a genealogist
Mushroom hunt with a mycologist
Dig for a day with an archaeologist
Back-to-back sessions with a psychologist

Topos of the Appalachian Trail
Floor plans of your house, to scale
Potpourri—inhale—exhale
The clear tones of a
nightingale

I'll shine and polish boots for you
Clean out your dresser drawers, too
Watch over baby, koochie koo
And promise always to be true

Four window washers for three hours
  A course to develop your healing powers
  CD, audio, and video towers
  "Green and pleasant English bowers"

Pecan, apple, cherry pies
  Contact lenses for your eyes
  Tai chi each morning at sunrise
  A listener while you rhapsodize

Allergy shots against achoos
    Your To-Do list wiped clean of Dos
    Jigsaws and crosswords to amuse
    Next time you're late, I will excuse

A barre where you can do your bending
    No more borrowing or lending
    Finish all that you have pending
    I'll tend whatever might need tending

At work, a permanent parking space
    Insight on the marketplace
    Leather, initialized briefcase
    A spritz of water in your face

*T*urandot, complete libretti
   A spontaneous shower of confetti
   Homemade gnocchi and spaghetti
   Grandma's crispy Apple Brown Betty

Star watch at the planetarium
   Snails and fish for your aquarium
   Exotic plants in a terrarium
   Next semester's books (I'll carry 'em)

Anagrams—challenge your brain
Dancing with a whooping crane
Jack Frost on the windowpane
Workouts with no pain, just gain

Choice shows only in prime time
Your business plan in pantomime
Curator's tour through the Guggenheim
Life's boring? Shift your paradigm

An island off the coast of Spain
Gently falling warm spring rain
Late Victorian gown and train
Jogging down a country lane

A hammock slung across a grove
A scuba dive for treasure trove
A passport and the will to rove
A live-in chef and Garland stove

A tiny house tucked in a dell
Picket fence and wishing well
Soy milk to raise your HDL
A pledge to never kiss and tell

A joystick for those games you play
   An outdoor fountain, fall, or spray
   A pillowy lounge at end of day
   Espresso cups, saucers, and tray

Umbrella when it mists or fogs,
Hails, snows, or rains cats and dogs
A pond swimming with pollywogs
Wassail! Wassail! Let's lift our nogs

A hike to St. Helena's crater
A cruise south of the equator
A cleaning of your carburetor
Reunion at your alma mater

African textiles bold and proud
Tell me what you think, out loud
The chutzpa to address a crowd
A riotous, rolling thundercloud

Sandpaper to smooth out the rough
  New closets to hold all your stuff
  A cozy, fluffy, fake-fur muff
  Encouragement when times are tough

Your favorite author's autograph
  A humorous play to make you laugh
  "Thank you! Thank you!" from your staff
  Wimbledon and Steffi Graf

A library of mysteries
   A winter's worth of antifreeze
   A rack of honeycomb (sans bees)
   A puppy from the pound (sans fleas)

A bronco-busting rodeo
   Clock alarm with radio
   Pedometer measuring heel and toe
   Spring flowers blooming in the snow

A newspaper full
   of good news
   An Hermès scarf of brilliant hues
   West Coast condo, West Coast views
   A week on a farm 'midst oinks and moos

NO MEDDLING

Rock-climbing and camping gear
All parking fines paid for one year
A barbecue, a keg of beer
A promise not to interfere

Ward off the chill, hot buttered rum
Your very own song to sing or hum
Warm croissants and jam (oh, yum!)
A classical guitar to strum

Data entry: five hours' worth
 For your horse, a leather girth
 A night of merriment and mirth
 Guard rails 'round the upper berth

Pole through tidal river rushes
 Acrylic paints, palette and brushes
 An oil field that only gushes
 Next two deals: royal straight flushes

AND
DITTO.

The Concorde to London on a whim
  Complete set of the Brothers Grimm
  A figure always slim and trim
  I'll row beside you while you swim

A set of foreign language tapes
  Flaming brandied cherry crepes
  New furnishings from couch to drapes
  Matching full-length opera capes

A year's supply of hand lotion
  A fast game of Spit in the Ocean
  My grandma's secret love potion
  (In case you get a certain notion)

A video of your life and times
  Wind indicator, sock, and chimes
  Gin and tonic, ice cubes, limes
  A bucket full of silver dimes

A day of dozing, dabbling, dreaming
Relaxing in a hot tub steaming
A week at work devoid of scheming
Creative juices flowing, teeming

A Renoir sketch, signed, framed, and dated
A birthday gift, somewhat belated
On moving day, house packed and crated
Your newest book critiqued and rated

Next semester's tuition paid
   Grandstand seats at the Rose Bowl Parade
   Jeans, already cut and frayed
   I'll always call a spade a spade

A flagstone patio and walk
   Let's fix the boat—I'll sand, you caulk
   Beach-house rental at Montauk
   Hang gliding with a red-tailed hawk

Aged, smoked Virginny ham
   Expensive French perfume (one dram)
   Shoreside bake, lobster and clam
   Thick sweater knit from woolly lamb

Lyrics for a sing-along
    Instructions and tiles for mah-jongg
    Doubles tournament, ping-pong
    I will admit when I am wrong

Four runs down a waterslide
    A totally magical mystery ride
    Camping à deux by the riverside
    Barefoot sailing on the tide

A fortnight roving Scotland's heath
    Movie-star bonding of your teeth
    A velvet-ribboned holly wreath
    With bayberries strewn underneath

First-aid kit and smoke alarm
    Fresh eggs and cheeses from the farm
    Pendant, brooch, bracelet, and charm
    Escort service, arm in arm

I'll render simple, higher math
    Help steer you down the proper path
    Sprinkle jasmine in your bath
    Take down your walls, plaster and lath

Carousel horse all set to prance
Rounds and lines of contra dance
Pen pal from the south of France
A new paint job for the old manse

Round-table lunch with your old flames
An address book (record their names)
Your near and dear in picture frames
The next Winter Olympic Games

Municipal bonds and blue-chip stocks
　Fireproof safe-deposit box
　First grade without chicken pox
　Tubs and tubs of purple phlox

Always the captain, always the skipper
　A foot to fit the right glass slipper
　At your well, a silver dipper
　Here's the remote—you be the flipper

The hills of Tuscany, a villa
Video movies—star: Godzilla
A string of fragrant beans, vanilla
For you, pardner, a sarsaparilla

Horseback riding on the trails
One of those cars that rides the rails
Screwdriver, hammer, wrench, and nails
A lawn mower that never fails

Gilded chairs found while antiquing
   Those obscure woodcuts you've
      been seeking
   A quickie course in public speaking
   Rid the floors of midnight creaking

Chart your cash flow at no fee
   Take up a hobby—Geography
   Read a Maggody mystery
   Explore virtual reality

A post-and-beam house in the pines
   An office chair that just reclines
   Tap-dancing gig with Gregory Hines
   A no-strings date who wines and dines

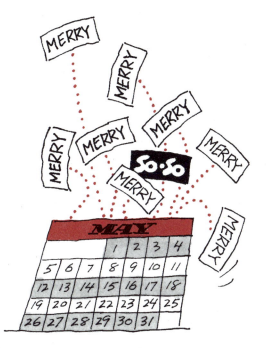

Braids of garlic, wreath of bay
   A swath of calico chambray
   Hand-caned chairs from old Bombay
   A mostly merry month of May

A box of exquisite bonbons
   Geisha girls and mama-sans
   Let bygones be just that—bygones
   Petition to bring back the Fonz

Someone to run your daily backup
   Leisure time so you don't crack up
   When tires go flat, your car I'll jack up
   Whatever's scattered, I will stack up

A limousine at your command
   The prettiest mirror in the land
   Manicure for foot and hand
   First trombone in a Dixieland band

Ballroom dance with a smooth mover
   Lessons in snowboarding maneuvers
   Replace those ancient drapes with louvers
   Cross-Canada train, Quebec-Vancouver

Ski-Doo ride o'er hill and dale
   Flashlights guaranteed no-fail
   Should we swamp: you steer, I'll bail
   Away, away with all junk mail

A ceiling fan to soothe and cool
   A free-form gunite swimming pool
   Your choice of fancy German tool
   Let me hand paint that kitchen stool

Jars of ginger, milk, and honey
   A parasol on days too sunny
   No groans when you are cute or punny
   Hearty laughs when you are funny

An essay on the op-ed page
   The ultimate job, a decent wage
   All your opinions judged as sage
   An hour to fret upon the stage

A date for double solitaire
   Shampoo, style, and dry your hair
   Pills to banish mal de mer
   Fireworks show extraordinaire

Chop cords of wood so you don't freeze
   Reconcile your checkbook, just say please
   On Arbor Day I'll plant ten trees
   Import a fresh Hawaiian breeze

Every day a compliment
   A cloudless night, the firmament
   Return to all things innocent
   The mettle to be different

King-size quilt plumped high with down
   Birthday bash, complete with clown
   A highfalutin designer gown
   One night, you pick it, on the town

Broadway hit, seats of your choosing
   Hot-glue gun when stuff needs fusing
   Insights gained when you're musing
   Spirit to win; good grace when losing

No glass ceiling left to shatter
   No questioning mind over matter
   Little feet sounds: pitter-patter
   Lunch with Alice's Mad Hatter

Exercise room complete with trainer
   Your next challenge: a no-brainer
   Pesto, pasta, tongs, and strainer
   A perfect from-the-top half-gainer

Massage your feet until they tingle
   Climb down your chimney as old
      Kris Kringle
   String bells to make your front door jingle
   When at your parties, I'll mix and mingle

Pick with a down-home Tennesseean
  Learn to fly a lake amphibian
  A private yacht on the Aegean
  Ten days snorkeling the Caribbean

Software and your own installer
  High, high heels to make you taller
  Piano rolls by the great Fats Waller
  Soundproof room to hoot and holler

Fly cast 'cross Scotland—guaranteed trout
  When angry, I'll subdue my pout
  Deck any guy who calls you stout
  Your shower leaks? I'll spread the grout

A day to savor spring's delights
   Dust off the bike, dig out the kites
   Explore the city, take in the sights
   Or shed your shoes, turn out the lights

Michael Jordan, one-on-one
   Stilts to add a little fun
   Panama hat to thwart
      the sun
   Deep-sea fishing off
      Galveston

A greyhound rescued off the track
A size-eight DK, off the rack
A Christopher Parkening CD pack
Traction when road ice turns black

Next movie rented, your selection
Mud bath and mask for smooth complexion
Attic to cellar home inspection
Put an end to vivisection

Lavender and rose sachet
Potting wheel, kiln, and clay
In-line skates—go out and play!
Madrid in the fall. Olé!

Rivers rife with pike and muskies
Trek Alaska (mush! you huskies)
A lift up when you're feeling dusky
Stair climber to reduce that buttski

Flat water and a rowing shell
   An incentive to excel
   The ability to spell
   Knowing left from
     right as well

Rocking chair and a bestseller
   From the pound, a hound named Yeller
   Sleight of hand with Penn and Teller
   Deep-sea diving with your feller

Geraniums crowding windowsill
   Rosemary, thyme, fennel, and dill
   L. L. Bean binge, I'll foot the bill
   I'll read aloud when you are ill

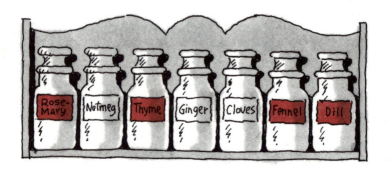

E-mail each day when I'm away
   A music box of cloisonné
   A jeweled egg from Fabergé
   Count on me, I'll never stray

A silver star atop your tree
   Rousing camaraderie
   Carolers caroling merrily
   Raclette of the finest Brie

A sixteenth-century Japanese scroll
   Fifty-yard-line seat at the Super Bowl
   First pick of the derby winner's foal
   OK, I'm game—let's rock 'n' roll

Two-hours-long long-distance chat
  Baseball mitt, shoes, cap, and bat
  Ankle weights and exercise mat
  Next weekend I will clean the flat

Travel folders to peruse
  Or put your feet up, take a snooze
  If you want, we'll sit and schmooze
  And listen to B.B. sing the blues

Every tooth the Tooth Fairy took
  The borrowed returned, from tool to book
  Justice wielded every crook
  If I'm a bore, employ the hook

From Savile Row, a tailored suit
　　Opponent points all rendered moot
　　Serenade of harp and lute
　　Choice wine, choice tenderloin *en croûte*

Golf clubs, spare time, and a pro
　　Dream-team foursome primed to go
　　Bobby Jones course, south, no snow
　　A handicap of two (you'll crow)

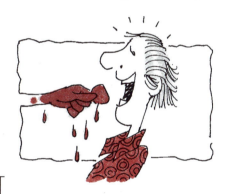

Hand-dipped chocolates for you, dear
　　Piano lessons for one year
　　Flowing scarves of white cashmere
　　Sweet nothings whispered in your ear

A place to volunteer your skills
Pro bono update of your will
A coffee cup that never spills
Relive, safely, life's old thrills

Maple syrup in the spring
A gold and garnet friendship ring
Karaoke sing sing sing
A two-days-in-the-country fling

Cool cellar stocked with vintage wines
Prospecting time in DeBeers's mines
Collection of my opening lines
Rope hammock swinging
'neath the pines

Pedestal table from Saarinen
The elegance of a Mont Blanc pen
The simple song of the winter wren
Ring in the New Year with Big Ben

The haunting sound of a wolf's howl
Deft moves when deboning fowl
Thickest, longest, Turkish towel
Scare burglars off: learn how to growl

Full-length hooded robe of terry
   Weekend in a monastery
   Rubbings from a cemetery
   Recycled paper stationery

A Ferrari and a pickup truck
   Fresh-from-the-field corn to shuck
   Strategically placed nip and tuck
   Prescience to know when to duck

A clear day above timberline
   A willing ear while you opine
   New house, built to your design
   Once a month, a valentine

Elocution lessons for your teens
    Repair windows, panes, and screens
    Recycle those old magazines
    Forget forever, angry scenes

Open up this place with skylights
    Give your hair a lift with highlights
    Leave work early, bask in twilights
    Count satellites on clear-sky nights

A burbling brook, a greeny glade
A chestnut tree to offer shade
First place in the motorcade
A velvet couch that will never fade

Stuffed animals—they don't need walking
  Five straight hours of no talking
  Rodeo Drive, shopping and gawking
  Chores accomplished—no balking

Touring bike, helmet, and shoes
  Gym membership, I'll pay the dues
    A lovebird pair, all bills and coos
    Chimney sweep to scour your flues

Barometer to gauge the weather
   Pocketbook of hand-tooled leather
   Walls faux marbled (paint and feather)
   A walk, just you and me together

Power suit and power shoes
   You present; I will enthuse
   You first's, go ahead's, after you's
   Some secluded rendezvous

July Fourth fireworks a-zooming
    Indoor plants forever blooming
    Creativity just booming
    On the horizon—nothing looming

CPA to compute your tax
    Bobeches to catch candle wax
    A nightshirt spun from golden flax
    La Costa Spa, now just relax

Tennis lessons with a pro
Ghost stories 'round a campfire's glow
Square dancing with a do-si-do
Your whole room hung with mistletoe

From Golden Gate to Liberty
Tour America sea to sea
Cape Cod, Chicago, Santa Fe
I'll chauffeur you the whole darn way